MICROSERVICES ARCHITECTURE

Learn Microservices FAST and EASY!

2nd edition

Copyright © 2015 by Kevin Watts.

Table of Contents

Introduction

Microservice architecture is used in large and complex software applications. The whole application is broken down into a set of services for ease of use, efficiency, as well as ease of understanding. The services of the application can contain communication mechanisms between one another, which is known as inter-process communication. This is normally by use of threads. However, microservices are prone to some challenges, including the performance itself. Before beginning to develop one, you need to be aware of these and seek for ways to handle them. This explains the need for monitoring your microservice which is also discussed in this book.

Chapter 1- Definition

In this book, we will go a step further and explore microservices in depth. Microservices need to establish a way that the client will be able to reach the different services it needs within the architecture. In some microservices there are dependencies which exist between the different services, while in others microservices there are no such dependencies.

There are numerous ways this can be done and these have been discussed in this book. Some microservice architectures only provide a single point of entry. This can easily be implemented by use of an API Gateway. We will continue to explore this concept in this book. Before venturing into the actual development of your microservice, you need to keep in mind how it will be monitored in terms of its progress. For instance, it is good for you to know how to react in case of overload to the microservice. You also need to understand both the users of the microservice and the partners of your system.

Chapter 2 - Java and Microservices

In Java, it is possible for programmers to create microservices.

Spring Boot

This makes use of an embedded server to easily and quickly create java applications. Java enterprise edition containers are not needed in this case since an embedded version of tomcat is used. With Spring Boot, components such as Rest services can be independently exposed. This is what is recommended in microservices architecture since in case some maintenance is needed, the whole of the system will not have to be redeployed. We now need to demonstrate this.

We will use maven 3 and Eclipse Luna. Three maven projects will be created for the purpose of demonstrating microservices. We will use these three projects, which are reusable APIs, as a symbol of back-end functionality. One of the projects will act as a consumer of the other two projects. The three projects will have the following names: P-backend, C-backend and O-backend and they will have no archetype. In the poms for our projects, we need to create a startup Spring Boot and REST services, so let us add dependencies as shown below:

```
<parent>
<groupId>org.springframework.boot</groupId>
<artifactId>spring-boot-starter-parent</artifactId>
<version>1.3.0.RELEASE</version>
</parent>
<dependencies>
<dependency>
<groupId>org.springframework.boot</groupId>
<artifactId>spring-boot-starter-web</artifactId>
</dependency>
<dependency>
<groupId>org.springframework.boot</groupId>
```

```
<artifactId>spring-boot-starter-jersey</artifactId>
</dependency>
</dependencies>
```

Now that we have established the dependencies, we can then get into coding. We will create a first class and give it the name "MyApplication". This class will be the same in all three projects. The reason for this is because it will act as the initiator to the Spring Boot. This is shown below:

```
import
org.springframework.boot.autoconfigure.SpringBootApplicati
on;
import org.springframework.boot.SpringApplication;
@SpringBootApplication
public class MyApplication {
public static void main(String[] args) {
SpringApplication.run(Aplication.class, args);
}
}
```

We will then create another class and give it the name "MyApplicationConfiguration". This is a resource configuration class, so we will use the "@Configuration" spring annotation to indicate this. In this case, our resource manager is "jersey". The REST service for the consumers will be exposed by this resource manager. If our application was real, we would have used this class for creation of data sources which will grant us access to the databases and other resources. However, we need you to focus on the Spring Boot, so we will use mocks for representation of the data access.

```
import org.glassfish.jersey.server.ResourceConfig;
import javax.inject.Named;
import
org.springframework.context.annotation.Configuration;
```

```java
@Configuration
public class MyApplicationConfiguration {
@Named
static class JerseyConfig extends ResourceConfig {
public JConfig() {
this.packages("br.com.first.project.rest");
}
}
}
```

Consider the class given below:

```java
import
org.springframework.context.annotation.Configuration;
import javax.inject.Named;
import org.glassfish.jersey.server.ResourceConfig;
import org.springframework.web.client.RestTemplate;
import org.springframework.context.annotation.Bean;
@Configuration
public class MyApplicationConfiguration {
@Named
static class JConfig extends ResourceConfig {
public JConfig() {
this.packages("br.com.first.project.rest");
}
}
@Bean
public RestTemplate restTemplate() {
RestTemplate rTemplate = new RestTemplate();
return rTemplate;
}
}
```

We will use the above class in the backend for the "Order".

We now need to implement the REST services. We first create a class which will provide the features for our customers. This should be done as follows:

```
public class MyCustomer {
private long c_id;
private String c_name;
private String c_email;
public long getCid() {
return c_id;
}
public void setCid(long id) {
this.c_id = c_id;
}
public String getCname() {
return c_name;
}
public void setCname(String c_name) {
this.c_name = c_name;
}
public String getCemail() {
return c_email;
}
public void setCemail(String c_email) {
this.c_email = c_email;
}
}
```

The REST service will have only two capabilities. One of the capability will query a customer using the "c_id" and the other one will query all the customers. This is demonstrated in the program shown below:

```
import javax.ws.rs.core.MediaType;
import java.util.List;
import java.util.ArrayList;
import javax.inject.Named;
```

```java
import javax.ws.rs.Path;
import javax.ws.rs.GET;
import javax.ws.rs.Produces;
import javax.ws.rs.QueryParam;
@Named
@Path("/")
public class CRest {
private static List<MyCustomer> Cs = new
ArrayList<MyCustomer>();
static {
MyCustomer c1 = new MyCustomer();
c1.setCid(1);
c1.setCname("First customer");
c1.setCemail("firstcustomer@gmail.com");

MyCustomer c2 = new MyCustomer();
c2.setCid(2);
c2.setCname(" Second Customer");
c2.setCemail("secondCustomer@yahoo.com");
MyCustomer c3 = new MyCustomer();
c3.setCid(3);
c3.setCname("Second Customer");
c3.setCemail("thirdCustomer@yahoo.com");
MyCustomer c4 = new MyCustomer();
c4.setCid(4);
c4.setCname("C Fourth Customer");
c4.setCemail("fourthCustomer@yahoo.com");
MyCustomer c5 = new MyCustomer();
c5.setCid(5);
c5.setCname("Fifth Customer");
c5.setCemail("fifthCustomer@gmail.com");
cs.add(c1);
cs.add(c2);
cs.add(c3);
cs.add(c4);
MyCustomers.add(c5);
}
@GET
@Produces(MediaType.APPLICATION_JSON)
```

```java
public List<MyCustomer> getCustomers() {
return cs;
}
@GET
@Path("customer")
@Produces(MediaType.APPLICATION_JSON)
public MyCustomer getCustomer(@QueryParam("c_id") long
c_id) {

Customer cli = null;

for (MyCustomer mc : cs) {
if (mc.getCid() == c_id)
cli = c_id;
}
return cli;
}
}
```

With the above, the REST service can be concluded. Now products which are associated with a certain customer can be searched using the customer id. Our services will be made up of the following classes:

```java
public class MyProduct {
private long p_id;

private String pk;
private String p_description;
public long getPid() {
return p_id;
}
public void setPid(longp_ id) {
this.p_id = p_id;
}
public String getPpk() {
return pk;
}
```

```java
public void setPpk(String pk) {
this.pk = pk;
}
public String getPdescription() {
return p_description;
}
public void setPdescription(String p_description) {
this.p_description = p_description;
}
}

import javax.ws.rs.core.MediaType;
import java.util.List;
import javax.ws.rs.Produces;
import java.util.ArrayList;import javax.ws.rs.GET;
import javax.ws.rs.Path;
import javax.inject.Named;
import javax.ws.rs.QueryParam;
@Named
@Path("/")
public class PRest {
private static List<MyProduct> ps = new ArrayList<MyProduct>();
static {
MyProduct p1 = new MyProduct();
p1.setId(1);
p1.setPpk("wxy1");
1.setPdescription("First Product");
MyProduct p2 = new MyProduct();
p2.setPid(2);
p2.setPpk("wxy2");
p2.setPdescription("Second Product");
MyProduct p3 = new MyProduct();
p3.setPid(3);
p3.setPpk("wxy3");
p3.setPdescription("Third Product");
MyProduct p4 = new MyProduct();
p4.setPid(4);
p4.setPpk("wxy4");
```

```java
p4.setPdescription("Fourth Product");
ps.add(p1);
ps.add(p2);
ps.add(p3);
ps.add(p4);
}
@GET
@Produces(MediaType.APPLICATION_JSON)
public List<MyProduct> getProducts() {
return ps;
}
@GET
@Path("product")
@Produces(MediaType.APPLICATION_JSON)
public MyProduct getProduct(@QueryParam("p_id") long
p_id) {
Product prd = null;
for (MyProduct pd : ps) {
if (pd.getId() ==p_ id)
prd = pd;
}
return prd;
}
}
```

The order service will be made of the following classes:

```java
import java.util.Date;
public class MyOrder {
private longo_ id;
private long o_amount;
private Date date_ordered;
private MyCustomer c;
private MyProduct p;
public long getOid() {
return o_id;
}
public void setOid(long o_id) {
this.o_id = o_id;
}
public long getOamount() {
```

```java
return o_amount;
}
public void setOamount(long o_amount) {
this.o_amount = o_amount;
}
public Date getDate_Ordered () {
return date_ordered;
}
public void setDateOrdered(Date date_ordered) {
this.date_ordered = date_ordered;
}
public MyCustomer getCustomer() {
return c;
}
public void setCustomer(MyCustomer c) {
this.c = c;
}
public MyProduct getProduct() {
return p;
}
public void setProduct(MyProduct p) {
this.p = p;
}
}

import javax.inject.Inject;
import javax.ws.rs.Produces;import java.util.Date;
import javax.inject.Named;
import javax.ws.rs.core.MediaType;
import javax.ws.rs.Path;
import javax.ws.rs.GET;
import javax.ws.rs.QueryParam;
import org.springframework.web.client.RestTemplate;
@Named
@Path("/")
public class ORest {
private long o_id = 1;
@Inject
private RestTemplate rTemplate;
```

```
@GET
@Path("order")
@Produces(MediaType.APPLICATION_JSON)
public MyOrder sOrder(@QueryParam("customerId") long
customerId,
@QueryParam("productId") long productId,
@QueryParam("amount") long amount) {
MyOrder order = new MyOrder();
MyCustomer c = rTemplate.getForObject(
"http://localhost:8081/c?id={c_id}", MyCustomer.class,
customerId);

MyProduct p = rTemplate.getForObject(
"http://localhost:8082/p?p_id={p_id}", MyProduct.class,
productId);
order.setCustomer(c);
order.setProduct(p);
order.setOid(o_id);
order.setOamount(o_amount);
order.setDateOrdered(new Date());
o_id++;
return order;
}
}
```

It can then be concluded that the Spring Boot provides a very powerful implementation of microservices architecture. The implementation itself is very simple but also very powerful.

Chapter 3 - Using an API Gateway to Build Microservices

Whenever you decide to build a microservice architecture, you need to come up with a way that the microservice will interact with the clients of the application.

Suppose that you are developing a shopping application to be used on mobile devices. Of course, you need to give information to the buyer about the details of each of the products that you are offering. This means that you have to develop a page for the product details. A good example of this is sort of page can be seen when you are buying an item on Amazon. Information about order history, reviews, basic product information, recommendation, inventory and shipping is provided.

When you open the Amazon page about the product on your mobile device, you will notice that a lot of information is given regardless of the size of the devices.

In a monolithic architecture, this application would have been implemented using a single REST call to the app. A load balancer would been used for routing a request to one of the instances of the applications which are all identical. Various database tables would have then been queried and the response, finally, relayed to the client.

However, with the microservices architecture, this would have been different because the data which is rendered on the product details page would have been shared by multiple microservices. The data shown on the product details page could be owned by the following microservices in this case:

Order Service- this will show the order history.

Catalogue Service- which can provide the basic details of the product such as name, price, and others.

Review Service- both positive and negative reviews from the customers.

Inventory Service- warning if the inventory is low.

Shipping Service- deadlines, costs and other information.

Recommendation Service- other items which are highly recommended.
Our aim is to come up with a way for the clients of the application to be able to access these services.

Client-to-Microservice Direct Communication

Theoretically, it is possible for a client to directly communicate with a microservice.
The microservice can possess a public endpoint in terms of a URL such as

"https://<service_Name>.api.company_name.endpoint_name".

The URL could be mapping to the load balancer which is responsible for the routing of requests to the instances of the available microservices. The client of the application must query all the above services for it to get all the details of the product.

However, this method is subject to a number of limitations. Notice that the client has to make requests to all of the services. What will happen if the application is too complex, especially in the case of large applications? If these requests have to be sent over a LAN, then these could have a negative impact on the network. The code used on the client side of the application needs to be about equal in complexity.

Refactoring of microservices also becomes difficult. As time progresses, it may be that the system needs to be changed, especially depending on how it has been partitioned. The application developer might decide to merge more than one service together or split up a single service. Due to the direct communication between clients and services, this becomes a difficult thing to do.

This is why it is not recommended for clients to perform a direct communication with the services. These problems can however be solved by use of an API gateway.

API Gateway

An API gateway provides a single entry point into a certain system. What it does is that it encapsulates the structure of the system and then provides an API which can be used by all the clients. The API can also be responsible for monitoring, caching, authenticating, request shaping and managing, load balancing, and static response handling.

The REST API is connected to the service. All requests which are sent from the clients will have to go through the API gateway. It then takes responsibility for routing, protocol translation, and composition. Each of the request is routed or forwarded to the correct microservice. The API gateway works by invoking multiple microservices simultaneously. The results from these microservices are then aggregated into a single result. It also has the ability to translate between different web protocols.

Each of the clients can be provided with a custom API by the API Gateway. In our example, for instance, a single request or query can be used to retrieve all the details of any of the products.

Netflix API Gateway is a good example of API Gateway use. This is available on different devices such as tablets, TVs, smartphones, and gaming systems. The API Gateway used in this case employs a device specific adapter code. This means that all kinds of devices are supported.

Advantages and Disadvantages of an API Gateway

The main advantage of using an API Gateway is that the internal structure of the application is encapsulated. The clients will just have to invoke the Gateway rather than invoking specific services within the application. Each of the clients is provided with a specific API. This greatly reduces the number of round trips necessary between the client and the application.

The main disadvantage associated with the use of an API Gateway is that the component has to be developed, deployed, and then maintained. This means that it can become a development bottleneck.

For the developers to expose each endpoint of the microservice they must keep updating the API Gateway on a regular basis. The updating process should be a lightweight one. If this is not the case, then the developers will have to wait and maybe in line so as to update the API Gateway. However, the advantages of using an API Gateway overwhelm the disadvantages, meaning that for most applications it is highly recommended for you to use the API Gateway.

How to Implement an API Gateway

When designing an API Gateway, there are some of the design issues which you should consider. These include the following:

Performance and scalability- most companies usually handle or service billions of requests in a single day. This shows how important the performance of the API Gateway is. The Gateway should be developed on a platform with the capability to support non-blocking, asynchronous I/O. If you need to implement an API Gateway which is scalable, then there are numerous techniques that you can use. On Java Virtual Machine (JVM), you can use frameworks such as Vertx, Netty, JBoss Undertow or Spring Reactor, which are all NIO-based.

NodeJS is an option which is not based on JVM and it is built on the Javascript engine of chrome. You can also choose to use NGINX and it will offer you a scalable, mature, high-performance server and a reverse proxy that is easily deployed, programmed, and configured. With NGINX plus, you can be able to control access to system, authenticate, load-balance requests, provide application-aware health checks, cache responses and performance monitoring.

How to use a Reactive programming model- the API Gateway just routes or directs requests to the right backend service. Other requests are handled by the invoking of multiple services which provides multiple results. These are then aggregated into a single result. In some cases, these requests are not related in any way, or they are independent of each other. For us to minimize the response time, then, it is necessary for us to process independent requests concurrently. However, it is possible for the requests to be dependent upon one another.

Validation of the request may be needed before routing or directing it to the backend service. If the API Gateway wants to fetch information about the details of the product, then it might begin by fetching information about that particular customer. Use of the traditional asynchronous callback method to write API Gateways is always prone to errors. A lot of complexity is also involved, meaning that the code will be difficult to be understood. To solve these problems, it is recommended that you write APIs in a declarative manner by use of the reactive approach. Examples of these include the Javascript promises and Scala features. Use of the reactive approach for writing APIs leads to simple APIs and very efficient ones. The API can also be supported on all the available browsers.

Service Invocation- since microservices applications are distributed, a means for inter-process communication needs to be established and then implemented. With the traditional approach, it could be easy for you to just handwrite the code. Inter-process communications are of two types. The first one involves using the asynchronous, message-based mechanism. Message brokers like AMQP or JMS are used in some of the applications. Others like Zeromq cannot be broken, and the services perform a direct communication.

Another inter-process communication mechanism is asynchronous, like in Thrift or HTTP. Most systems will make use of both mechanisms, that is, synchronous and asynchronous. Notice that these two mechanisms each have multiple implementations. Most applications usually make use of these implementations during their development time. In this case, the API Gateway should be prepared or developed in such a way that it can be able to support a variety of communication mechanisms.

Service Discovery- the API Gateway should possess a mechanism to know the location of each of the microservices with which it communicates. The location in this case is in terms of the IP address and a port. In the traditional system, this could be done by just specifying the location of the hardware. However, in a modern microservice application which is cloud-based, this is impossible or non-trivial. Some of the services of the infrastructure such as the message broker usually have a static location. To specify the location of these, we can simply use the variables of the OS environment. However, it is difficult for you to determine or locate the location of a microservice.

This is because their locations are dynamic, meaning that they keep on changing. Also, due to upgrades and autoscales, the set of the instances of a particular service will keep on changing. This explains the need for the API Gateway to use a service discovery mechanism. This can be either a client-side discovery or a server-side discovery mechanism. In this case, you need to understand that the system will use the client-side discovery mechanism. The API Gateway will then have to query the Service Registry. The service registry contains all the instances of the microservices together with their locations, meaning that it is like a database.

How to handle partial failures- this should be taken care of during the implementation of an API Gateway. In a distributed system, when a certain service calls another service and then it fails to get a response, or the response is slow, then a partial failure is said to have occurred. However, blocking should never occur even when the API Gateway is waiting for a downstream service. To handle the failure, it all depends on the kind of service which has failed or the scenario that caused the failure. In case a single service has failed to respond, the whole system should not fail. This means that the client should get a response from the rest of the services since they are important.

The failed service can be left empty or replaced with a default service. However, if all the microservices fail, then the API Gateway should return an error to the client of the application. Caching of data is also important. If the microservice failed, then the cached data can be returned to the client. A good example is the price of the product, which might keep on changing. If the service responsible for providing the price fails, then the API Gateway can return the cached price to the client. The API Gateway itself can be used for caching or the caching can be done on an external cache like the Memcached or Redis. If the user or client gets the default or cached data, then this is an indication that user experience is not affected by failures.

With Netflix Hystrix, which is a library, it is possible for programmers to write code with the ability to invoke or call remote services. It has a mechanism so that a call can be timed until they reach a certain threshold. It is very efficient because the client or the user will not have to wait for a service which is not responsive or not available.

This is implemented by use of a mechanism similar to how a circuit breaker works. If the number of errors for a particular service exceeds the set threshold, then all of the requests will fail, but for a short period of time. This is done by the use of the circuit breaker. An action is provided so that it can be executed in case a particular service fails. For those using Java Virtual Machine (JVM), it is highly recommended that you use this library. In case you are using a non-JVM environment, then you can look for a library which is similar to Hystrix.

To conclude, it is good for you to implement an API Gateway in microservice based applications. This will provide only a single entry into the system. The Gateway will take over the role of routing of client requests, translation of protocols and composition. Each of the clients of the application are provided with a custom API. Failures can be masked by using an API Gateway, since it has the capability to return cached or default data in case a particular service fails.

Chapter 4 - Using NodeJS and MongoDB to Build Microservices

It is good for developers to use NodeJS for building microservices due to the following reasons:

The demo version of microservices is I/O intensive rather than being computing intensive. This makes NodeJS a better system since it is event-based.

The number of open source components that can be used together with NodeJS are numerous.

All of its components are evented. This includes all the default client libraries and every node module. Examples of the components include MySql, MongoDB and couchDB.

It is a lightweight framework and it is possible for the developer to choose the components that you need most rather than having a huge framework.

We now want to explore the scheduler. This is built using NodeJS. It uses the REST full API to expose the functionality and it acts like a JOB scheduler. Consider a situation where you want to send some information to certain people in particular on a daily, weekly, monthly or yearly basis. This can be done by use of this scheduler, in which the report will be sent automatically on your behalf. This is a microservice because it has been used to perform a single job and it does it in the way it was requested to do so. For the sake of having a persistent storage, MongoDb will be used to back it.

As shown in the above figure, each of the subfolders performs or provides a functionality which is different from the others. If back up is needed, it is done using additional Javascript. The following section provides a further explanation on these:

Config- all configuration related settings are placed in this folder. The file "index.js" is responsible for exposing it and files such as devConfig.js are responsible for backing it. They have a specific setting for the development environment.

Controllers- we should have different controllers which will then be used to expose the resources like a REST full API. schedulerController forms the main point of entry to get all the JOB requests and then pass them over to our JOB scheduler module.

Data- this forms the data access layer.

Global- it represents all the events which are global. It also provides a platform for setting up the initial infrastructure.

Jobs- it must be there for the job action to execute whenever the scheduler invokes them. You can use this for the purpose of sending emails or to get data from sources which are external. However, it will depend on what you need.

Scheme- it defines the structure for the request for the JSON.
Dockerfile- this is used when deploying in the containers. It acts as the docker.

gruntfile.js- it enables or enhances the productivity of development tolls when used together with GRUNT tool.

package.json- NPm uses this for management of NodeJS packages.

server.js- it forms the entry file for the NodeJS.
For the purpose of managing packages, the file "package.json" is used. The following code for the file is used for management of the scheduler microservice:

```
{
"name": "SchedulerService",
```

```
"version": "0.0.1",
"description": "",
"main": "server.js",
"scripts": {
"test": "echo \"Error: no test specified\" && exit 1"
},
"keywords": [
"scheduler",
"service"
],
"author": "Mike Artemov",
"license": "IDC",
"dependencies": {
"agenda": "^0.7.12",
"body-parser": "^1.4.0",
"express": "^4.7.1",
"jsonschema": "^0.5.0",
"mongoskin": "^1.3.4",
"underscore": "^1.0.0",
"winston": "^0.6.3",
"winston-mongodb": "^0.3.5"
},
"devDependencies": {
"grunt": "^0.5.5",
"grunt-nodemon": "^0.3.1"
}
}
```

The following modules have been used:

Agenda- used for all JOB schedulers which are CRON-based.

body-parser- used to parse HTTP post JSON data.
express- used to build the REST full service.

jsonschema- used to define and validate a JSON request

mongoskin- used to interact with MongoDB

underscore- used for JavaScript utility functions

Winston- used to log in the infrastructure

winston-mongodb- used by MongoDB for transportation of Winston logging infrastructure

dev dependencies- it restarts the system whenever a change is made to the Javascript file. It is used together with the GRUNT tool nodemon.

For the sake of developing activities, we need to use GRUNT tools. They provide developers with a huge number of tools. When working with NodeJS, most developers prefer to use nodemon. With this, in case a change is made to the Javascript file, the whole system is restarted. To validate files which are related to Javascript, you can use "jshint". It also provides quality to your Javascript code. The following is a sample code for GRUNT configuration tool file:

```
module.exports = function (grunt){
grunt.initConfig({
nodemon: {
all:{
script: 'server.js',
options: {
watchedExtensions: ['js']
}
}
}
});

grunt.loadNpmTasks('grunt-nodemon');
grunt.registerTask('default', ['nodemon'])
};
```

The above code is used by the scheduler microservice. From the configuration, it will use nodemon and then restart in case a change is made to the Javascript file. Thescript "server.js" is responsible for this.

"Jshint" file is also well liked by developers. It is used to detect and catch errors in case they occur in your code. Examples of these errors include those associated with variables, such as the use of the ones which are not defined. It is highly recommended that you catch these errors at a very early stage. Failure to do this will lead to serious issues when it comes to debugging the system at a later stage. The file also provides you with numerous options which you can use to detect and solve errors of different kinds.

Using the Docker to Deploy Microservices

Microservices are good when it comes to scaling. They can also have their own independent cycles which can scale when needed. These require many resources to function. Docker is widely used in Linux-based systems and it is just a light weight container technology. The platform is open-source mostly used by system administrators and developers for the purpose of building, running and shipping of applications which are distributed. Docker also provides a cloud service called "Docker Hub". This is used for automating and sharing workflows.

It works by using Linux CGroups so as to provide the required isolation of the resources such as the network, CPU, memory, and block I/O. Docker was developed using the Go programming language which belongs to Google.

You now have a full understanding of the Docker. We need to build a microservice based on NodeJS and it will act as a docker container. It will be deployable on various environments such as production and staging.

In the NodeJS scheduler-service project, you will find a file named "Dockerfile". Its code should be as follows:

```
# DOCKER-VERSION 0.10.0
# Pull base image.
FROM ubuntu:14.04
# Install Node.js
RUN apt-get update
RUN apt-get install -y software-properties-common
RUN add-apt-repository -y linux/node.js
RUN apt-get update
RUN apt-get install -y nodejs
ADD . /src
RUN cd /src; npm install
ENV PORT 3001
```

```
ENV NODE_ENV development
EXPOSE 3001
#CMD ["node", "/src/server.js"]
```

The above file contains all the instructions which are necessary for one to build a Docker container image. From the instruction written "FROM", we will be able to use Ubunti 14.01 as our image. The rest of the instructions are to be used for installation of NodeJS. The NodeJS file will be copied to a folder named "src". An "npm install" will also be done after navigation to the "src" folder. Notice that the NodeJS file is copied from the current location of the Dockerfile to where the new image will be created. With the above code, all the files within the package "package.js" will be installed. The port with the number 3001 will also be exposed to the container. The last line of the code defines the instruction to be executed once the container has been executed. In the case above, the command is a node command. It will be responsible for starting the node application.

How to deploy the scheduler service

If you need to deploy your scheduler service, follow the instructions below:

Begin by building the Docker container image. Navigate to the location of the Docker file via the command line. After that, just run the following command:

sudo docker build -t <username>/<name_of_image>

You can then run the Docker container:

sudo docker run -p 3001:3001 -d <username>/<name_of_image>

With the above command, the internal port number 3001 will be mapped to the external port with the number 3001. This means that the service will be listed in the external port numbered 3001.

Mac and Windows users

We said that Docker was developed by using the Go programming language which belongs to Google. Its kernel makes use of Linux features. This makes it impossible for us to use on a Mac or Windows system. However, it is supported in virtualized environments. This means that it can be used inside an instance of EC2, virtualbox or Rackspace Virtual box. However, if you are using Mac or Windows, it is highly recommended that you use it together with Boot2Docker or with Vagrant.

Docker Hub

Docker hub provides a cloud service through which you can automate workflows and share applications. Some people are tired of building containers for different machines. This problem can be solved by use of the hub. With this, you just need to build a single hub and then pull the image which has been built to different services. You can then run the services after that. It integrates very well with Bitbucket and Github. If the git repo for your nodejs application is managed with these services, the repo can be linked to a docker hub through an online service. Build command can then be run so as to directly build the image from the repo. Continuous integration can be achieved by use of minimal effort when using the docker hub cloud service. The automated workflow provided by the hub can also be leveraged. The figure below shows a section of the docker hub build screen:

How to Scale a Microservice Running on a Docker Container

With a Docker, it is possible for us to deploy the services in a reliable manner. However, the Docker is not a software-deployment mechanism which is full-blown. This means that it is hard to scale microservices which are built in the Docker container. However, there are multiple ways we can achieve scaling. To do this, you can use open source PaaS tools such as Flynn and Deis. These will help you to scale your Docker containers.

You are now aware of how to use tools such as NodeJS and Docker, which are open source software for development of microservices.

Chapter 5 - QBit Microservice

QBit is a framework which is solely based on microservice. In this chapter, we will create an example of a QBit framework. We will use QBit and gradle.

When using QBit to develop a microservice, the process is easy and fast and yet one can achieve a lot at the same time. With QBit, we can develop both in-memory and asynchronous services. We will use Gradle to create a standalone application which will be available via the REST/JSON API. It will also be possible for you to curl the example. A command line utility named curl can be used for this purpose.
Example:

To know the size of the TODO list, run the following command:

curl localhost:8080/services/todo-service/todo/count

If you need to add a new TODO item, run the following command:

curl -X POST -H "Content-Type: application/json" -d '{"name":"abc","description":"abc"}' http://localhost:8080/services/todo-service/todo

The Build file for Gradle

If you need to easily run the sample app and then generate artifacts which are executable, then you should use Gradle. The gradle build file is as follows:

```
group = 'io.ad.qbit.samples'
apply plugin: 'idea'
apply plugin: 'java'
apply plugin: 'm'
apply plugin: 'application'
version = '0.2-SNAPSHOT'
sourceCompatibility = JavaVersion.VERSION_1_8
targetCompatibility = JavaVersion.VERSION_1_8
sourceSets {
main {
java {
srcDir 'src/main/java'
}
resources {
srcDir 'src/main/resources'
}
}
}
mainClassName = "io.ad.qbit.vertex.http.Test"
repositories {
mLocal()
mCentral()
}
dependencies {
compile group: 'io.ad.qbit', name: 'qbit-vertex', version: '0.6.1'
compile "org.slf4j:slf4j-api:[1.7,1.8)"
compile 'ch.qos.logback:logback-classic:1.1.2'
testCompile group: 'junit', name: 'junit', version: '4.10'
}
idea {
project {
jdkName = '1.8'
```

```
languageLevel = '1.8'
}
}
```

Notice that you have to install gradle on your system. There are gradle plugins for both IntelliJ and Eclipse.

With QBit, you can turn Java POJOs into JSON very easily and without any annotations. However, you need to understand that the gradle file will seem to be more complex compared to the java file.

The TODO file for our example should be as follows:

```
import java.util.Date;

public class TDItem {
private final String desc;
private final String name;
private final Date deadline;
public TDItem(final String desc, final String name, final Date deadline) {
this.desc = desc;
this.name = name;
this.deadline = deadline;
}
public String getDesc () {
return desc;
}
public String getName() {
return name;
}
public Date getDate() {
return deadline;
}
}
```

Java service for TODO

The TODO service will be as follows:

```
package io.ad.qbit.samples;
import                io.ad.qbit.annotation.RequestMethod;import
io.ad.qbit.annotation.RequestMapping;
```

```java
import java.util.List;
import java.util.ArrayList;
@RequestMapping("/todo-service")
public class TDService {
private List<TodoItem> tdItemList = new ArrayList<>();
@RequestMapping("/todo/count")
public int size() {
return tdItemList.size();
}

@RequestMapping("/todo/")
public List<TodoItem> mylist() {
return tdItemList;
}
@RequestMapping(value        =        "/todo",        method        =
RequestMethod.POST)
public void add(TodoItem it) {
tdItemList.add(it);
}
}
```

Notice that we have used "RequestMapping". This will work in the same way as Spring MVC REST annotations. It will provide us with a subset of what is provided by Spring MVC. Whenever anyone posts to the "/todo" URI, then the "add" method will be called.

The service must be started first before you can run it. This is done by use of the "ServiceEndPointServer". This can be started very easily. You can use a service bundle to specify different threading models. This will make the service in the thread either run in the same or in different service threads.

QBit makes use of apartment model threading for the services. An efficient queuing mechanism is used so that the amount of handoff between the service threads and the IO threads is reduced.
The main method should be as follows:

```java
package io.ad.qbit.samples;
```

```
import io.ad.qbit.server.ServiceEndpointServer;
import io.ad.qbit.server.EndpointServerBuilder;
public class TDMain {
public static void main(String... args) {
ServiceEndpointServer s = new
EndpointServerBuilder().build();
s.initServices(new TDService());
s.start();
}
}
```

With "EndPointServerBuilder", you can specify the NIC Interface and the port number that you want to use for binding your service.

The services will be available over web socket or over REST. You need to have installed gradle to be able to run this service. Consider the gradle command shown below:

gradle run

The above command will generate an idea project. Consider the next command:

gradle run

With the above code, an example from gradle will be run.
Due to the use of gradle, it will be easy for us to distribute any zip files.

Chapter 6- Monitoring Microservices

When monitoring whether microservices have been passive, tools like Nagios can be in use.

User Experience and Microservices Monitoring

For microservices which change on a regular basis, you can try to migrate from certain features to others to assess the impact on the experience of the users. If you notice a weakness with your application, then you can take some time and improve it. Multi-variant testing and A/B testing can be used to assess the effect of combining different features. To monitor a microservice doesn't mean that you sit and wait for a failure to occur. There is a need for you to know more about the users. This includes knowing what they like and what they dislike.

Debugging and Microservices Monitoring

Statics and metrics for runtime are very critical and especially in distributed systems. Remote calls are highly used in microservices architecture. In microservices, the factors which need to be monitored include available memory, request per second, expired tokens, failed authentication, tokens and connections. You need to understand these parameters to be in a position to monitor and debug your code. However, you need to know that working with distributed systems is not an easy job. This means that it will be crazy for you to work with a microservice without reactive monitoring. With reactive monitoring, it will be possible for you to react in case a failure condition occurs in the system.

Microservices Monitoring using Circuit Breaker

To prevent the occurrence of catastrophic cascades, it is highly recommended that you make use of the circuit breaker. The trigger in this case can be set to the reactive microservice monitoring. For the case of downstream services, consider registering them with the service discovery. With this, you will be able to mark nodes as unhealthy. In case outages occur, you will have the capability to react by reroute. What we need to avoid as much as possible in this case are cascading failures. In case the main service fails, you can react by providing a deprecated service or data to ensure availability of the service.

Public Microservices and Microservices Monitoring

Everyone wants to monitor the runtime statics for a particular application. Although it is good for you to trust your partners, you need to use microservices monitoring so as to verify this. Once you have made your microservices to be partner available or publicly available, then you need to rate limit or monitor them. For those who have used the public REST API from google, then you have a good knowledge about the Rate limit. It works by limiting the number of connections that you should establish. This feature is good when you want to limit the number of requests from a certain client with a particular id. This is normally done per unit of time.

If you have deployed a particular microservice to be either public or partner accessible, then you need to use this feature. If you fail to do this, then the microservice might be prone to a disaster. This can give you stress. To avoid this, make sure that you monitor your microservices that you publish. You also limit how they are accessed.

Microservices Libs for Microservices Monitoring

There are microservices libraries that can be used for microservice monitoring. QBit can be used for this purpose. It comes installed with a runtime statics engine that can be used for the monitoring of microservices. Querying and using this statistics engine is a very easy task. In case the services forms a cluster, then this engine will be able to keep their statics. The code that you write will be capable of reacting to the metrics of the microservices. The stats from QBit can be used for implementation of features such as rate limiting and spinning of new nodes whenever it is detected that there is a possibility for overloading to occur. These stats can also be fed into the StatsD.

StatsD and Microservices Monitoring

StatsD is a network daemon which is used fior aggregating some statistics such as timers and counters. It then ships these statistics to backend services. There are several client libraries through StatsD for programming languages such as python, java, node, ruby and others. The server for StatsD uses a published wire protocol to collect statics from the clients. For the capturing or collection of information from the clients to happen, you must implement this in your code. You will then be in a position to collect the data and then report it where necessary. StatsD collects this data overtime and then reports it for monitoring and analysis on a periodic basis. The data must be flushed to the monitoring engine that you choose to be the best.

It is widely used for monitoring of microservices due to the simplicity involved when using it. The client libraries that it uses are very small, and it cannot lead to cascading failures. You need to check for other alternatives which can work with QBit other than StatsD. There are several of these.

Reactive Microservices Monitoring

In microservices architecture, reactive monitoring is essential. You will need to make use of this in working with your partners, debugging, knowing who your users are and in building of reactive systems. Reactive systems should react to load and handle failures without cascading any outages. You should note that this is not a hindsight decision. When building a microservice, you need to keep in mind the idea of reactive monitoring from the start.

The microservices library that you use for the purpose of development should have the capability of supporting this. If it has the ability to monitor the runtime statistics, all the better. Reactive monitoring is the core of microservices library. You should avoid using microservices libraries which do not support this feature. Code Hale and StatsD statics will help or enable you to easily gather metrics in a very standard way. To build dashboards once you have understood the data, you can use tools such as Kibana, Graphite, Banana and Datadog. QBit, which is a Java microservices library supporting querying of statistics and it can be fed into Code Hale stats.

The library has numerous uses since it can be used for creation of reactive features for the purpose of either spinning up new nodes or for creating reactive features.

You now know how to monitor your microservice architecture and the importance of doing so. You can know your users, know who your partners are, and know how your system will react in case an overload occurs.

Conclusion

In the world today, the software used in companies for automation of processes are large and complex. This means that it becomes impossible for most people to understand the code used to develop this system. The functionality of the system also becomes a difficult task for the users to understand.

This explains the reason why we need to make use of the microservices architecture when developing our large and complex systems. However, the architecture is not limited to applications which are large and complex. It can still be used in applications which are simple and small. In this case, the developer might be interested in making the application easy to understand or to make it easy to operate.

You need to monitor your microservice in terms of how it operates. You need to know who your partners are as well as the users of your application. You also need to know how to react in case overload to your microservice occurs. There are numerous varieties of software that can be used to do this. You should identify the correct one and then do what is necessary. It is possible for you to create microservices with java programming languages. Most programmers prefer to use Spring Boot to do this. This is why it has been explored in this book. With Spring Book, you will use an embedded version of a server, meaning that you will not have to use java enterprise edition libraries. An API Gateway can also be used to implement a microservice. With this, the application that you create will provide only a single entry into it.

You can combine NodeJS and MongoDB to develop a microservice. The resulting application will provide intensive I/O operations rather than being computing intensive.

This is why programmers like to use this framework for creation of microservices. My hope is that the book will help to gain a deep understanding of microservices and be in a position to create a microservice.